Jesus 911

*Effective Prayers to
Reclaim Your Life*

Larry and Marion Pollard

Jesus 911: Effective Prayers to Reclaim Your Life

Copyright © 2019 by Larry and Marion Pollard

All rights reserved. No portion of this publication may be reproduced, stored in a retrieval system, or transmitted in any form by any means—electronic, mechanical, photocopying, recording, or any other—without prior permission from the publisher.

Scripture quotations marked (TLB) are taken from The Living Bible copyright © 1971. Used by permission of Tyndale House Publishers, a Division of Tyndale House Ministries, Carol Stream, Illinois 60188. All rights reserved.

Scripture taken from the New King James Version®. Copyright © 1982 by Thomas Nelson. Used by permission. All rights reserved.

Scripture quotations from The Authorized (King James) Version. Rights in the Authorized Version in the United Kingdom are vested in the Crown. Reproduced by permission of the Crown's patentee, Cambridge University Press

Scripture quotations taken from the New American Standard Bible® (NASB), Copyright © 1960, 1962, 1963, 1968, 1971, 1972, 1973, 1975, 1977, 1995 by The Lockman Foundation. Used by permission. www.Lockman.org

Scripture quotations are from the ESV® Bible (The Holy Bible, English Standard Version®), copyright © 2001 by Crossway, a publishing ministry of Good News Publishers. Used by permission. All rights reserved.

ISBN: 978-0-578-59180-3

Table of Contents

About the Authors _____ 1

Introduction _____ 4

Section One _____ 17

Section Two _____ 61

Section Three _____ 119

Note from the Authors _____ 139

About the Authors

Larry and Marion were high school sweethearts, married young, and began their family. Neither had experienced the "perfect childhood" with the white, picket-fenced home and doting parents. Their generational histories included alcoholism, abandonment, adultery, multiple divorces, poverty, and sexual and physical abuse. However, they determined to change those things within their own family. Knowing they could not make these changes on their own, they adopted their own philosophy of, "We will do the best we can and ask Jesus to make up the rest."

As faithful members of a very conservative church, Larry was always drawn into leadership and Marion became his support staff of one. Of all the things they thought they would do (teaching, ministering, missionary work), deliverance and casting out demons was certainly never on the horizon. This was not a topic of discussion or teaching in their conservative arena.

Jesus 911

After moving from West Texas to the Dallas/Fort Worth area, Larry (a plumber, heating and air conditioning specialist) determined he would go back into business and told Marion to start looking for a truck for him. But Marion recounts, "It was like Jesus came and sat down beside me and told me, 'You are not to get him a truck. He is not to go into business. I will be his mentor.'" Larry never questioned if she had heard from the Lord. He knew in his heart she was right.

They established their ministry, "Comfort Ye My People," in 2002. While the ministry looks different now, it has always been about helping people find freedom and a closer relationship with Jesus Christ. And while they never sought out a name for themselves, marketed the ministry, or took credit for anything the Lord does for those who come, thousands of people have come to the Pollards for prayer.

Over the years of the Lord's mentorship, study of the Scriptures, and experience, they have formulated groups of prayers that take care of the vast majority of an individual's deliverance. "After that we just have to dig a little deeper," Larry reflects. *Jesus 911: Effective Prayers to Reclaim Your Life* is a self-help tool for an individual or group to have and use the prayers for their freedom in Jesus.

Introduction

It is a proven fact that in times of crisis or desperation, more people turn to Jesus through prayer, going to church, or reading their Bible than during any other time. In times of crisis, people are willing to do anything to get spiritual help for their earthly dilemma. Also, during times of desperation, some people seek to know Jesus for the first time in their life or make a new dedication to Him. However, in many situations, Jesus is the last resort—tears, cries for help, remorse, promises (that won't be kept), all to get Jesus' attention. Curses, Satan, demons, and traumas have taken all that is valuable. They've caused torment, bad health, broken relationships, and destroyed everything. In order for you to reclaim your life, find happiness, restore family relationships, and get out of poverty you have to do your part, and Jesus promises to do His part for you. The prayers in *Jesus 911* will give you a great start.

Larry and I have ministered through prayer since 2002. As students of God's word we are open to His teachings, we invoke the Holy Spirit, and we believe that Jesus died on the cross for our sins. Our belief in Jesus as the Son of God ensures our salvation. The Holy Bible is our source and our textbook for understanding curses, demons, and trauma.

There are people who consider the Torah (the first five books of the Bible) as the only word of God. However, others believe the Old Testament isn't relevant and only the New Testament is needed because Jesus fulfilled the prophecies of the Messiah. Larry and I believe the whole Bible is relevant—both Old and New Testaments. The older books contain different requirements for dealing with sins, repentance, forgiveness, and blessings since they were written prior to the life, death, and resurrection of the ultimate sacrifice, Jesus Christ.

Larry and I have been faithful, churchgoing Christians all our lives, but we never experienced any teaching regarding curses and demons.

Jesus 911

Although they are found throughout the entire Bible, Satan must have blinded our eyes (perhaps yours too) to the Scriptures dealing with curses and demons and what we should do with them. It was not by choice that we began the ministry of deliverance. We did not seek it out. The Lord just threw us into it. We both have a heart for helping people, but neither of us ever imagined deliverance ministry was what the Lord had in mind for us.

When we first began to minister in the area of deliverance, Larry read, studied, sought out mentors, and prayed. (For my part, I mostly prayed and prayed and prayed in the beginning years.) People would come, the Lord would show up and do the deliverance, teach us something new, and people would be set free. Larry describes his job as, "A glorified can opener." He "opens the can" and then the communication between the Lord and the individual begins. There are many ideas about deliverance from curses and demons and how it should be done. Our ministry is entirely based on the Holy Scriptures in the Bible. The Lord does the work and

He gets the glory and praise—*we just do our part.*

When we pray, we expect God will put all things together, into place, making all things whole and making all things the way we *perceive* they should be. We cry out, "Lord, heal my illness," or "help my child to resist the temptations of drugs, sin, and evil," or "get me out of this situation and I promise to go to church." The truth is that Jesus can do all of these things because He is merciful, caring, loving and orderly. We can trust Him.

In all areas of breaking curses, legal deliverance, and inner healing give God the glory and honor (take none for yourself). Recognize Jesus Christ of Nazareth as your deliverer, healer, intercessor, and redeemer. Acknowledge the Holy Spirit for helping lead you through the process of reclaiming your life from Satan. Thank God for His victory and His warring and ministering angels and their assistance. "Put on the whole armor of God that ye may be able to stand against the wiles of the devil. For we wrestle not against flesh and blood, but against principalities, against powers, against the rulers of the darkness of this world, against spiritual wickedness in high places. Wherefore take unto you the whole armor of God" (Ephesians 6:11–13, KJV). You can do nothing on your own. You must have Jesus!

Your Part

You have a part to play in your freedom. It was your sinful choices or the acts of others that got you into the mess. Now, you have to make another choice. The choice to never return to these sins or allow traumas to control your mind. Holding onto that choice is what will keep your healing and deliverance. It is hard to fight the enemy of the Lord. Your enemy, if we only have part of ourselves to fight with. We are weak humans. We need every part of us to be whole to fight back. Therefore, breaking curses, deliverance, and inner healing can be the answer to gaining your strength. Be diligent to stay close to the Lord as you walk out your healing.

There are consequences for your sins. You

must repent, be forgiven and be redeemed. Repent means to turn away from. You must turn away from your sinful acts. This will require you to fight your flesh and desires. This does not mean you will not transgress and lose all the ground you capture. It does not mean that you will not be forgiven. It *does* mean that you have now opened the doors to the enemy, and they must be closed. Go back to the area of Legal Deliverance and pray the prayers. Close the door and give no ground to the enemy.

"Call to Me and I will answer you, and I will tell you great and mighty things, which you do not know" (Jeremiah 33:3, NASB). You can make that call and expect Him to hear you and answer. The Lord's ways are not our ways. Time is in His hands.

As you read this book, identify your sins, ungodly soul ties, unforgiveness, and those of your previous generations. Pray the prayers and be specific. Allow the Holy Spirit to lead you. When you identify a pattern in your life that you can recognize as a curse, go back to that section and break that curse. The more you pray, the more the Holy Spirit will reveal, and the more healing and freedom you will have!

Note: Before you begin, there are three prayers we recommend you pray for yourself and those participating in prayer with you. If you stop and come back to read and pray, repeat the three prayers.

Establish Authority

By reading and speaking the prayers aloud, you not only have the power of the actual *prayer,* but you also have that power reinforced when you hear yourself praying and speaking. So be bold and pray aloud! This prayer will establish authority in *all* parts of the spirit, soul, and body according to the Scriptures. Luke 10:17 reads, "Then the seventy returned with joy, saying, 'Lord even the demons are subject to us in Your name'" (NKJV). In Matthew 18:18 Jesus says, "Assuredly, I say to you, whatever you bind on earth will be bound in heaven, and whatever you loose on earth will be loosed in heaven" (NKJV). And in John's gospel we read, "And in that day you will ask Me nothing. Most assuredly, I say to you, whatever you ask the Father in my name He will give you" (John 16:23, NKJV).

Begin Prayer:

Our Father, I thank You that You loved me before I was formed in the womb. I thank You that You had high and holy purposes for me even before I was born. I command demonic, evil, and unclean spirits, including all evil spirits that are empowered by curses and/or controlled by curses under Satan's authority, that they shall not interfere spiritually, mentally, and physically with me. You will not cause any pain or any fear in any and all parts of the spirit and soul (saved and unsaved), including both the inside and outside of my body. You shall not cause any confusion, slumber, sleep, restricted verbal communications, or physical distractions, including pain.

I now command all that are under Satan's authority to stop and desist now. You will stand down and not hinder my free will in any way for this time of prayer, repentance, and deliverance. I now command and release all bound evil spirits (if necessary).

I now command and bind the Strong Man's hands with a three-cord rope that is not easily broken. The Strong Man is now blinded and gagged and will be identified by his bound hands. He will not interfere with this deliverance. His legal right to me and my family is broken, and he will immediately go to the feet of Jesus or to the pit, never again to return.

I now command and declare the kingdom of God is and shall be established here on earth as it is in heaven at this time and at this location." As Matthew 6:10 says, "Your kingdom come. / Your will be done / On earth, as *it is* in heaven" (NKJV).

Purpose:

We have come to do the business of God's kingdom by establishing the blood, the word, and the cross.

Protection and Submission

Begin Prayer:

Thank You Lord for Your Son, Jesus Christ, and for His blood atonement upon the cross. Thank You, Lord for Your protection and mercy. We plead the blood of Jesus Christ over

- everyone here today/tonight;
- all parts of our spirits, souls, and bodies;
- door posts, from every corner, above, below, and all around this place;
- our loved ones, family members, extended family, our animals, and every good gift the Lord has given us, wherever they may be.

We thank You, Father, for Your Holy Spirit and for the anointing that breaks the yoke so the captives can be set free. We now submit to the Holy Spirit and ask the Holy Spirit for help to reveal all things necessary for the freedom promised by Jesus Christ for our lives. We thank You Father for Your holy angels. We ask that You station Your warring angels and Your ministering angels here to help with this deliverance.

Prayer Command Directed Against Satan

Begin Prayer:

Satan, I now address you in the name of Jesus Christ, who is my Lord. I speak to

- the principalities and powers;
- the rulers of the darkness of this age;
- the spiritual hosts of wickedness in heavenly places;
- the demons, the devils, evil and

unclean spirits, fallen angels and any other names or titles you have taken upon yourselves or have been given by others.

I declare that my Lord Jesus Christ totally conquered you at the cross when He triumphed over you and when He held you up to public ridicule. My Lord now has all authority and all power in heaven and on earth, and He has given me the authority to use His name. In Jesus' name I speak to all that are under Satan's authority and control, and I command you

- not to manifest, blaspheme, and lie;
- not to communicate with each other;
- not to communicate with any entity above, below, and around you;
- not to hold hands, and you cannot hold onto each other;
- to turn loose from each other now;
- to disentangle yourselves from one another now;

Jesus 911

- to line up and leave when I command, dismiss, or release you, or your legal right is broken.

When you are commanded, dismissed, and released you will immediately leave this area and go to the feet of Jesus to become His footstool or wherever I direct, and you shall never return to this individual (insert name here: _____) or their dwelling place. All evil spirits who have *no legal right* to (insert name here: _____) are now dismissed and released to leave. In Jesus' name, get up, get out, and go! Go to the feet of Jesus!

Note: Repeat three or more times with a strong voice. Allow a brief pause to allow time for release. If there is no immediate release, understand they will have to go and maybe over a time period of days.

Section One

Strawberry Curses

What do strawberries and curses have in common? Surprisingly, quite a lot. A single strawberry has over 200 seeds. The seeds of a strawberry are visible on the outside, and they reproduce through vining. Larry and I have never seen a person with only one curse (maybe not 200 either), but curses are visibly manifested on a person (poverty, addiction, health, bitterness, etc.) and often reproduce from generation to generation.

The purpose of this workbook and prayers is to present you with information on different types of curses and demons, how they impact your life, and how to get rid of them. Larry and I hope to give you a deeper understanding of curses and demons based on our personal ministry experiences and Scripture references while also removing your anxieties and fears on the subject. Further, we will biblically address the different types of curses while empowering you with the tools you need to pray effectively to break these curses. Most of all, we want to give you a positive "pat on the back" for your desire to take charge of and reclaim your life.

Along the way, we will give you explanations of terms that may be unfamiliar to you, a little biblical history, and a few insights into experiences we have shared with clients. Certainly you are not alone when it comes to having challenges but looking for the source and doing something about it takes courage. In your church, you may not have been taught about invoking the power Jesus gave you to deal with curses and demons.

Not all curses have demons attached to them. However, if the demons have a "legal right" because of unrepented sin, the curse can carry demons. Someone must take ownership of the sin(s) (your own sins and the sins of their generations), repent, ask for forgiveness, and ask for the Lord's blessing. This repentance of sin breaks the legal right of an attached demon. The curse is broken through the acknowledgement of the curse, the repentance for the sin, the forgiveness of sin through Jesus, and the request made to the Lord for the curse to be broken.

The Sins of Adam and Eve

But of the tree of the knowledge of good and evil you shall not eat, for in the day that you eat of it you shall surely die (Genesis 2:17, NKJV).

Once we had a group of elders and a pastor from a church we attended over for dinner. During the dinner they asked, "Do you think that what my great-great-great-grandparents did could cause a curse or give me a demon?" Since we are still paying for the sins of Adam (to work the fields), Eve (painful childbirth), and the serpent (to crawl on its belly), and still suffering death, our answer was—yes! If you believe that the sins of Adam, Eve, and the serpent still cause us misery today, then you cannot eliminate the other generational sins and curses that would follow the family blood line.

The most common curses include biblical, generational, digested, and spoken curses (both self-curses and curses spoken by others). Demons can be connected to a curse but can also stand alone or as part of a group. You can be set free by breaking the curse and/or the legal rights of a demon through recognition, ownership, repentance of sins (yours and your ancestors), and forgiveness. By invoking the power of Jesus and the authority He has given you, you can close the ungodly spiritual doors that have been opened in your life by speaking and applying the prayers in this book.

In the following sections we provide you with prayers that break curses. These prayers are effective. Through the grace of Jesus, your faith, your trust in Him, your humility before God the Father, and your total honesty, these prayers will give you more freedom in life than you have experienced. Often, we are asked if this will break the curse off my children. Our belief is that the answer depends on the age of the child. We believe it does break the curse off your children if they are under the age of accountability (age 12 scripturally). If they are over 12 and under your authority, then include their name in the prayer as you come before the Lord. Adult children need to understand and pray for themselves, and a spouse needs to pray the prayers for themselves.

Could I Be Cursed?

A better question is, "How can you not be cursed?" Over the years, we have discovered that types and sources of curses are extensive. There are biblical curses, generational curses, digestive curses, self-curses, curses by others, witchcraft (occult) curses, and others.

Do any of the following apply to you or your family?

- Poverty and financial insufficiency
- Bareness/Impotency together with miscarriages and related male and

- female complications
- Failure of plans and projects and feeling your destiny met with disaster
- Untimely and/or unnatural deaths
- Sickness and disease, especially chronic and hereditary diseases
- Life traumas; going from one crisis to another
- Mental and emotional breakdowns
- Breakdowns of family relationships, including divorce
- Spiritually hindered in hearing God's voice, sensing God's presence, understanding the Bible, or lack of concentration in prayer and being devoid of spiritual gifts

If you answered yes to two or more of the above statements, then you have your answer. Yes, you are cursed. It stands to reason that the more you answered yes to the above statements, the more you are cursed. Further, the more you answered yes to both yourself and your family, the more you can identify generational curses. However, you cannot blame all the trouble or bad things in your life on your ancestors or family. We are all held responsible for sins we commit that open the doors to curses and demons.

Biblical Sin Curses and Digested Curses

The first time you heard the words "biblical sin curse," you most likely furrowed your brow, wrinkled your nose, and questioned what that meant. Biblical curses are rarely spoken of in the church from the pulpit or studied in a Bible study class. Be assured, they are as real today as they were in the times of the Old and New Testament writings. The truth is that most of us when reading the Bible don't recognize "curses" or how they affect us. Many generational sins begin with a family member committing a biblical sin which then follows the soul and bloodline DNA.

One of the foremost causes of a curse is the sin of disobedience to God's word. This invokes a "biblical sin curse," and demons can use this as an open door for oppression. It is not only if we have sinned and are under a biblical curse, but we also inherit the biblical curses for the sins of our fathers and forefathers including our mothers and foremothers. Biblical curses can be identified or appear as generational curses.

Rebellion is a curse and easily recognized within the generations. (See Jeremiah 28:16–17). Any occult practice, divination, sorcery, omens, witchcraft (shamans or curanderos), consulting a medium (psychic), and consulting the dead (Leviticus 20:2, 27; Deuteronomy 18:9–13) create curses. Changing the word of God to entice another person to believe a false religion, worshipping idols, and unforgiveness are also examples of *a biblical sin curse*. Deuteronomy 13:6–9 and Revelation 22:18–19 clearly state that you shall not take away from or add to the Word of God. How often is this done to promote a "new" religious following? Too many times to name!

Example: When a child is conceived or born out of wedlock, you can be sure that someone in the family before them had an illegitimate child and someone before that and so on and so on. In the family bloodline, someone sinned, and the biblical curse began. Deuteronomy 23:2 reads, "One of illegitimate birth shall not enter the assembly of the Lord; even to the tenth generation none of his descendants shall enter the assembly of the Lord." Does this mean someone of illegitimate birth cannot enter the church? No! It is a curse, not an unforgiveable sin. This curse can be broken by acknowledging the sin, repenting, and asking forgiveness.

Realistically, do you think that no one in 10 generations will commit this same sin? However, when they do sin, the 10 generation count begins again. The purpose of the following prayer is to cover or expand the breaking of biblical curses. So, let's begin breaking these curses by praying the following prayer.

Prayer For Removing Biblical Sin Curses

Begin Prayer:

In the name of Jesus Christ and with the sword of the Spirit, I now break and cut away all biblical sin curses, including all curses that have manifested as

- illegitimacy;
- mental and emotional breakdowns;
- repeated or chronic sickness (especially hereditary);
- barrenness, miscarriages, female or male physical issues;
- broken relationships including family, friends, and marriage(s);
- continuing financial insufficiency;
- being "accident prone";
- suicides and unnatural or untimely deaths in the family.

I/we repent and ask for forgiveness for our family and myself for violating the Word of God, knowingly or unknowingly. We have suffered the penalties of the biblical curses. I embrace Jesus Christ at the cross and give Jesus all biblical sin curses, including those that carry the death penalty, with demons, evil spirits, or the dead.

Galatians 3:13 tells us that Christ has rescued us from the curse pronounced by the law. When He was hung on the cross, He took upon Himself the curse for our wrongdoing: "For it is written in the Scriptures, 'Cursed is everyone who is hung on a tree'" (NLT). Thank you, Jesus. Blessed is Your Name.

Every demon, devil, unclean spirit by any name, function, or purpose attached to a biblical sin must leave now and go to the feet of Jesus. I have taken ownership of these sins, repented for me and my family, and have asked for forgiveness. The enemy no longer has any legal right to me or my bloodline, since Jesus carried every curse to the cross. In Jesus' name, get up, get out, and go! Go to the feet of Jesus!

Note: Repeat three or more times with a strong voice. Allow a brief pause to allow time for release. If there is no immediate release, understand they will have to go and it may be over a time period of days.

Scripture References for Biblical Sin Curses

- "One of illegitimate birth shall not enter the assembly of the Lord; even to the tenth generation none of his descendants shall enter the assembly of the Lord" Deuteronomy 23:2 (NKJV)
- Any occult practice, divination, sorcery, omens, witchcraft (shamans or curanderos), consulting a medium (physic), and consulting the dead: Leviticus 20:2, 27; Deuteronomy 18:9–13

- Teaching rebellion against the Lord: Jeremiah 28:16–17
- Idolatry through either the making or worshipping of an idol: Exodus 20:5; Deuteronomy 17:15
- Adultery: Leviticus 20:10; Numbers 5:27; Deuteronomy 22:22–27; Job 24:15–18
- Cruelty to a handicapped person: Deuteronomy 27:18
- Dishonoring one's parents: Deuteronomy 27:16
- Sexual relationship with an animal: Deuteronomy 27:21
- Defrauding one's neighbor: Deuteronomy 27:17
- Homosexual relationships: Genesis 19:1–25
- Sexual intercourse during menstruation: Leviticus 20:18
- Rape: Deuteronomy 22:25

- Accursed objects in your possession: Joshua 7:13
- Murder for hire (including paid to perform an abortion): Deuteronomy 27:25
- Murder: Deuteronomy 11:28; 27:24
- Forsaking the Lord: Deuteronomy 28:20
- Presumption in thought so that one disregards God's Word and devises their own way: Deuteronomy 29:19
- Cursing or mistreating Abraham's seed: Genesis 12:3; Numbers 24:19
- Enticing others away from the Lord into a false religion: Deuteronomy 13:6–9
- Taking away or adding to the Word of God: Revelation 22:18–19
- Refusing to warn sinners: Ezekiel 3:18–21
- Perversion of the gospel of Christ: Galatians 1:8–9

- Refusal to forgive others after asking God to forgive you: Matthew 18:34–35
- Child sacrifice, including abortion: Leviticus 18:21; Deuteronomy 18:10
- Disobedience against any of the Lord's commandments: Deuteronomy 11:28; 27:26

Digested Curses

Digested curses are curses that come through eating or drinking anything that you or someone else has prepared to impose a scheme or plan to do you harm. There are cultures where the local "doctor" is a witch or witch doctor (shaman, curandero, diablo). We have all seen the pictures and movies of witches at Halloween mixing a cauldron of some potion. We have ministered to many people in various social groups where they would go for a potion to conceive a child, murder someone, heal someone, or make someone fall in or out of love. You've heard of things being put in someone's drink so they can be taken advantage of. Some people knowingly do this type of thing to themselves through drugs (prescription or illegal drugs) and alcohol.

(Please note: Based on the definitions below we are not saying all medications or those who prescribe or prepare them are evil.)

Pharmacy (n.) late 14c., "a medicine," from Old French farmacie "a purgative" "use of drugs, medicines. *potions, or spells; poisoning, witchcraft*; remedy, cure,"

Prayer for Removing Digested Curses

Begin Prayer:

With the sword of the Spirit I cut and break away all digested curses by me or my family line. I repent and ask forgiveness for my sin and the sin of my family. I apply the blood of Jesus Christ over myself. John 6:56 states, "He who eats My flesh and drinks My blood abides in Me, and I in him"

(NKJV). I apply this Scripture to all digested curses that were voluntarily or involuntarily taken and/or forced upon me, both orally or sexually and knowingly or unknowingly, with potions, powders, food, or drink including spiritual and satanic rituals that required drinking blood, eating strangled meat, and cannibalism. The blood of Jesus Christ will now flow and cleanse all parts of my spirit, soul, and every area of my body, inside and out, of all demonic rights and curses created by digested curses. Thank you Lord Jesus for healing and cleansing my body and forgiveness of sin.

I now address any demon, devil, or unclean spirit attached to digested curses. "In Jesus' name, get up, get out, and go! Go to the feet of Jesus!

Note: Repeat three or more times with a strong voice. Allow a brief pause to allow time for release. If there is no immediate release, understand they will have to go and maybe over a time period of days.

Communion

After you have prayed, we recommend that you take communion (partake in the Lord's supper) and declare the following: "The flesh and blood of Jesus Christ will now flow throughout my body, cleansing and healing the damage and influence of all ungodly digested curses."

Generational Curses

After the birth of a baby, parents, family, and friends immediately begin to identify physical characteristics that resemble the mother and father or grandparents: smile, eyes, dimples, ears, nose, fingers, and toes. As the child grows, the generational physical features are easy to see along with their generational character. Generational characteristics begin to show up as their personalities develop.

However, there will be positive character traits and negative traits that are noticeable as well. Comments from family and friends might include mentions of a good student, a sweet spirit, a real beauty, loving, athletic, musical, artistic, and others. But of course there are also those (including from mothers and fathers) who add to the development of the child's character with negative comments such as, "You are going to be an alcoholic just like . . . you're going to marry over and over again just like . . . you have anger issues just like . . . you're never going to have an extra dime!" Again and again, the negative generational identity is reinforced through word curses such as these.

No one will ever convince me that someone really, deep in their heart, wants those negative, hurtful, and traumatic behaviors for their child. There is no way a child has made the poor decisions or choices that created the bad actions that affect them. Most negative behavior traits can be traced back to family members' behaviors from generation to generation—*generational curses*. We have discovered abusive men that were abused, and the abuser was abused, and they were abused. To date, I cannot remember the *first* abuser ever coming to our office, or the *first* rape victim, or the *first* alcoholic, or the *first* chronically ill, or the *first* to have an abortion or illegitimate child.

A Kiss from the One True Love

Remember the story of *Sleeping Beauty*, with the fairies that blessed the princess and the evil fairy who in anger cursed the princess? Consider this story (with a happy ending, praise the Lord) and how many of the issues that people struggle with today are a part of this story: abandonment, anger, broken relationships, poverty, control, digested curse (poison), deceit, vanity, witchcraft, early death, and more. The last fairy was able to change the *conditions* of the curse of death on the princess. The curse could only be broken by a kiss from her one true love.

The curse placed by the evil fairy could be broken once the conditions were met—a *kiss* from the one true love. Generational curses can be broken by your first love, the lover of your soul—*Jesus Christ*. However, there are some conditions that are required (just like the kiss). First, *Jesus must be your personal Lord and Savior.* You must be humble and willing to accept the responsibility of the generations before you for their sins and your own that brought the curse. You must repent on their behalf and yours, and ask for forgiveness and a blessing from the Lord. Is it really that easy? Yes. However, there still may be consequences and need for breaking of demonic legal rights that are attached.

What is a Legal Right?

Legal right is the demon's right to torment, stay, manifest, or cause harm because of a sin committed that has not been forgiven because the sin has not been confessed, there has been no repentance, and there has been no request for the Lord's forgiveness. Exodus 34:7 reads, "Who will by no means clear the guilty, visiting the iniquity of the fathers upon the children and the children's children, to the third and the fourth generation" (ESV).

Note: Demons attached to generational curses may or may not leave at this time. If you personally have given legal right to a demon by committing the same ancestral sin, you must personally break that legal right and command the demon to leave.

Example: There is an ancestral curse and demon from spilling innocent blood (occult worship, abortion, murder), and you have committed that same sin: there can be an ancestral "Strong man" (demon). If this is the situation, you must break the personal, legal right you have given the demon as well.

Confession is Made

Larry and I recommend that you pray this (and all prayers) aloud with a Christian witness present, in accordance with James 5:16, "Confess *your* trespasses to one another, and pray for one another, that you may be healed. The effective, fervent prayer of a righteous man avails much" (NKJV).

Further, we suggest that each person have a notepad to write down any problems with any words, symbols, names, paragraphs, or sins, especially for each generation as we count 1–30. Document any issues you experience either physically or mentally when saying these prayers. The brief pause following each paragraph is to allow the Holy Spirit to reveal any related issues that may require attention.

Please Note: It is very important *to finish the last sections* of these prayers and pray each section, including all words. After the prayers and for the next several weeks, document what you experienced, both positive and negative.

It is normal for the Lord, over time, to show specific areas that need more prayer. As you pray and curses are broken, any demonic attachment will be broken and have to leave when using Jesus' name. Demons will leave through any bodily orifice such as the watering of eyes, yawns, burps, popping of ears, urination, or stomach gas. Before you begin, shut down all distractions, including phones.

Breaking Generational and Occult Curses

The following generational prayer, "New Beginnings," is based on the Scriptures from Daniel 9 and prayers for breaking curses from Freemasonry and other occults. This prayer is not to be interpreted that it is coming against a person. Instead, this prayer is to break the lies and curses of the organization's mysticism and spirituality.

Instructions

In the space below, insert your full legal name/names (include your birth name, adopted name, nicknames, and any/all married names). This is for the purpose of identification when a sin was committed.

Begin Prayer:

I_____ am determined with all my strength to humble and submit all of my spirit, my soul, my mind, my heart, and my body to the Holy Spirit to glorify and raise Jesus Christ of Nazareth up, so to fulfill Deuteronomy 6:5: "You shall love the Lord your God with all your heart, with all your soul, and with all your strength" (NKJV).

I recognize God is merciful according to His Word (Jesus) as I repent and turn from my wicked ways. God, You were justified in Your actions against me and my generations and we have paid the penalties. I plead for the mercy of God to fall upon myself, my family, my ancestors, my people groups, my tribes, and my nation for my verbal confession that I make now. To the Lord, our God, belongs mercy and forgiveness. I ask Jesus Christ to intercede and to turn the anger, the fury, and the great evil away from us, including all curses, all rights of evil and unclean spirits, and all vows, oaths, and dedications made to Satan and his organizations.

I humbly request

- that You would incline Your ear to hear my prayers;

- that You would hear my pleas and supplications;
- that You would cause Your face to shine upon me and my generations, including the sanctuary of the Holy Spirit within me;
- that You would open Your eyes to see my pain and suffering including the thoughts and intents of my heart;
- that You would look upon my desolation manifested financially, physically, and spiritually;
- that You would remove all curses that are in Your Word, including all curses spoken against us;
- that You would forgive the sins, transgressions, and iniquities for me and for all my generations;
- that You would remove any wrath and dissension among my family members;
- that You (Jesus Christ) will be my kinsman redeemer and hear my prayers.

I ask that the Holy Spirit and the Lord Jesus would be strength in my weakness, to reveal now and in the future all areas that need repentance for myself and for my father, my forefathers, and my mother's generations, including all involvement with tribes, people groups, nations, false religions (including secret societies and secret organizations), worshipping demons, and being involved with Satanism and witchcraft, including rebellion. I do confess and repent for our stubbornness, iniquities, transgressions, and sins that we have done wickedly by departing from God's law knowingly and unknowingly. I also confess that we have disobeyed your Word, Jesus Christ, and the Holy Spirit.

I take full responsibility for my ancestors and accept the infirmities of _____ (name every infirmity or illness you know; cancer, heart problems, lung problems, etc.), confusion, shame, curses, death penalties, insanity, poverty, and all abominable acts, including using the Holy Bible to swear by, sexual acts and perversion, vows and judgments, and any curses that I, my family, and my ancestors have spoken over ourselves and others; and I now declare with the sword of the Spirit, the curses above shall be broken and cast down and covered with the blood of Jesus Christ.

I take ownership of the curses that have been poured upon me and my family from God's Word, for I know that God is not a liar and cannot lie. I take ownership also of all curses that attached to our family bloodline, including those spoken by the lineage of our own ancestors back to Adam and Eve. I do condemn the tongue that has risen up against me, our family, and our ancestors according to Isaiah 54:17, because of others that have placed curses upon us. Now, with the sword of the Spirit I break, cut away, and cast down all devices, all methodologies, all attachments, all assignments, all curses, and all enforcers from this day forward to have no more power, including legal rights, and shall be covered with the blood of Jesus Christ of Nazareth. I now bless those that we have hurt and damaged, including all the families, the individuals, and their children's children past and present to be restored, to be brought close, and to receive all good things that belong to them, especially intimacy and salvation through Jesus Christ.

I especially repent for our wicked ways and ask for forgiveness for myself, my family, my ancestry, my tribal groups, and my nations for

- causing pain, hurt, and suffering to myself and to those made in God's image;
- causing little ones to stumble, including all of God's creation (animals, insects, etc.);
- spilling innocent blood (killing), sacrificing human beings (including babies) by maiming and mutilating, rape, incest, torturing, recruiting others into ungodly and satanic organizations, rituals, and cannibalism;
- direct and/or indirect actions of betrayal that brought harm and

destruction to individuals, to the body of Christ and its leadership, including gossip, lying, introduction of false doctrines and rumors, or by agreeing with and glorifying Satan in the church by actions and deeds;

- manipulating, controlling, and engaging others to act, including myself, to participate contrary to God's Word that contributed to the destruction of the Bride of Christ (The Church);

- engaging in false religions and movements back to Babylon (Masons, Catholicism, Satanism, Mormonism, Hinduism, Buddhism, Islam, Kabbalah, New Age Religion) and all self-idolatry and practices that have developed and existed from Adam and Eve (including all worship of the creation, little gods, the heaven and the stars, the sun and moon, the seasons) and everything that was worshipped except the true God of Abraham, Isaac, and Jacob;

- engaging in the occult, which includes witchcraft, to have power over people's heart, emotions, spirit, soul, minds, and bodies;
- engaging oaths that we made to evil spirits and satanic organizations, including the use of blood, drinks, food, and secret rituals, including blood packs and agreements, to cause harm to our physical bodies, including our future generations and to others;
- closing down my spirit, my soul, my heart, and my emotions, including my conscience, so that I could not hear Abba Father, Jesus Christ, and the Holy Spirit.

I repent, renounce, and ask forgiveness for all the evil charged against myself and my family for presumptuous sins and for sins of ignorance, including:

- All the things that are known
- All the things that are unknown
- All words we have spoken, asking to join and partake with pagan ungodly secret organizations including their members and all associations with Freemasonry, Mormonism, Satanism, the occult, and false religions
- Blaspheming and mockery of my Heavenly Father, the Word of God, Jesus, and the Holy Spirit
- Believing and teaching others a false gospel

Please forgive us and remove all curses that I and my ancestors have spoken, on both the male and the female side, who swore and made oaths and vows using the Bible and the Words of the Bible to engage in any and all curses that ask You, our Heavenly Father, Jesus Christ, and the Holy Spirit to enforce. With the sword of the Spirit (the Word of God, Jesus Christ), I now break and cut away all obligations, swearing on the Bible, and kissing the Bible that obligated Abba Father, Jesus Christ, and Holy Spirit by our own free will to enforce including all male and female organizations that are related to such by various names.

The Prayer of Release

Begin Prayer:

Father God, Creator of heaven and earth, I come to You in the name of Jesus Christ, Your Son. I come as a sinner seeking forgiveness and cleansing from all sins committed against You and others made in Your image. I honor my earthly father and mother and all of my ancestors of flesh and blood, and of the spirit by adoption including godparents, but I utterly turn away from and renounce all their sins. I forgive all my ancestors for the effects of their sins on me and my children.

Jesus 911

True, Creator, Holy God, in the name of the true Lord Jesus Christ, in accordance with Jude 8–10, Psalm 82:1, and 2 Chronicles 18, I request You to move aside all celestial beings, including principalities, powers, and rulers, and to forbid them to harass, intimidate, or retaliate against me and all participants in this ministry today.

I confess and renounce all of my own sins, known and unknown. I renounce and rebuke Satan and every spiritual power of his affecting me and my family, in the name of Jesus Christ. I also ask that You prevent and forbid these beings, of whatever rank, from sending any level of spiritual evil as retaliation against any of those here, or our families, our ministries, or possessions.

I renounce and annul every covenant made with death by my ancestors or myself, including every agreement made with hell, and I renounce the refuge of lies and falsehoods that have been hidden behind.

In the name of the Lord Jesus Christ, I renounce and forsake all involvement in any organization, craft, or occult by my ancestors and myself. I also renounce and break the code of silence enforced by any occult on my family and myself.

I renounce and repent of all pride and arrogance that opened the door for the slavery and bondage to afflict my family and me.

I now shut every door of witchcraft and deception operating in my life and seal it closed with the blood of the Lord Jesus Christ. I renounce every covenant, every blood covenant, and every alliance with any spiritual powers behind it made by my family or me.

In the name of Jesus Christ, I rebuke, renounce, and bind witchcraft, the principal spirit behind occults, and I renounce and rebuke Baphomet, the Spirit of Antichrist, and the spirits of death and deception.

I ask the one true Creator Holy God to give me the gift of faith to believe in the true Lord Jesus Christ, as described in the Word of God.

I also renounce and rebuke the spirit of prostitution, which the Word of God says has led members of all occult organizations astray and caused them to become unfaithful to the one true and Holy God. I now choose to return and become faithful to the God of the Bible, the God of Abraham, Isaac, and Jacob, the Father of Jesus Christ, who I now declare is my Lord and Savior.

I renounce the insecurity, the love of position and power, the love of money, the greed, and the pride that would have led my ancestors into sin. I renounce all the fears that have held me or my family members such as: fear of death, fear of men, and fear of trusting. In the name of Jesus Christ.

In the name of the Lord Jesus Christ, I now take the delegated authority given to me over every spirit of sickness, infirmity, curse, affliction, addiction, disease, or allergy associated with all these sins that I have confessed and renounced, including every spirit empowering all iniquities and curses inherited from my family.

I exercise the delegated authority from the Risen Lord, Jesus Christ, over all lower levels of evil spirits and demons that have been assigned to me, and I command that all such demonic beings are to be bound together with chains of the blood of Jesus Christ, to be separated from every part of my humanity, whether perceived to be in the body or trapped in the dimensions, and they are not permitted to transfer power to any other spirits or to call for reinforcements.

Note: On a sheet of paper as you begin the next section of this prayer, please note which generations (and what you hear in your mind when the Holy Spirit reveals to you) that need to be addressed with individual prayer and repentance and identification of the sin. The Holy Spirit may reveal even more generations than these spoken.

Jesus 911

Instructions

Pause after each generation. As you repent, ask forgiveness, and confess each generation starting with my generation #1 (pause), generation #2 (pause), generation #3 (pause), generation #4 (pause); continue to speak out each numerical generation to the 30th generation. After the 30th generation ask forgiveness all the way back to Adam and Eve (grouping the generations together).

Example of a Generational Curse

The curse of Elisha on his servant Gehazi from the story of Naaman, a commander in the king's army with leprosy. Naaman was told to go and see Elisha, a prophet of the God of Israel, and he would be healed. Naaman went to see Elisha, taking gifts of money and clothing. Elisha would not come out of his house to meet Naaman. He sent his servant Gehazi to give Naaman a message. "Go, wash yourself seven times in the Jordan, and your flesh will be restored and you will be cleansed." (2

Kings 5:10, NIV). Though offended, Naaman finally did as Elisha had instructed and was cured.

To show his gratitude, he went back to Elisha's home offering the gifts. Elisha refused them. Elisha's servant chased after Naaman and lied about there being a need for the money and gifts for some others seeking Elisha's help. Generously, Naaman showered them upon Gehazi. Gehazi took them for himself, hid them, and later lied to Elisha about what he had done. Elisha's response: "'Naaman's leprosy will cling to you and to your descendants forever.' Then Gehazi went from Elisha's presence and his skin was leprous—it had become as white as snow" (2 Kings 5:27, NIV).

Leprosy and other diseases (cancer, headaches, arthritis, etc.) can be traced to generational curses or a self-inflicted curse. The curse will continue generation to generation until someone in the bloodline acknowledges there was sin, asks for forgiveness of the generations, repents, and asks for the disease to be broken.

Note: If you are a Freemason seeking release, or if you are a descendant of Freemasonry or any auxiliary or extension associated with Freemasonry, you may want to read and pray the prayers in the booklet Unmasking Freemasonry: Removing the Hood Wink, by Selwyn Stevens (Jubilee, 2007).

Concluding Prayer

Begin Prayer:

Holy Spirit, I ask that you show me anything else I need to do or to pray so that I and my family may be totally free from the consequences of generational sins.

Now, Lord our God, please redeem us, my family, and their children's children for 10 generations from all evil, blood guilt, sacrifices, and demonic worship. With Your mighty hand lead me in Your truths and Jesus Christ will be glorified this day. My God, incline Your ear and hear and open Your eyes and see my desolations, for I do not present the supplications before You because of my righteous deeds, but because of Your great mercies. As I present myself to You, Lord, hear, forgive, listen, and act!

Do not delay, for me and my family that are and will be called by Your name. Please, Jesus Christ, receive my offerings of verbal confession, of identification, ownership, and repentance as I lift up all iniquities, transgressions, sins, curses, oaths, vows, and judgments to Jesus Christ at the cross so that You will grant us peace, holiness, and restore our covenant blessings, as in Galatians 3:13: "Christ has redeemed us from the curse of the law, having become a curse for us. (for it is written, 'Cursed *is* everyone who hangs on a tree')" (NKJV).

I command, in the name of Jesus Christ, for every evil spirit to leave me now, touching or harming no one, and go to the feet of the Lord Jesus Christ, never to return to me or my family and children, siblings, and parents. I command that you now take all your memories, roots, scars, works, nests, and habits with you. I surrender to God's Holy Spirit and to no other spirit all the places in my life where these sins, transgressions, curses, and iniquities have been.

"Neither do I condemn you," Jesus declared. "Go now and leave your life of sin" (John 8:11, NIV).

Note: When you return to a sin *knowingly*, you will reopen the door that the demon for this sin entered. This is what the devil is waiting for. After your initial deliverance, you should expect spiritual warfare and temptations, including thoughts that are not your own. You have Jesus! He wins! Do your part and fight the enemy. Don't give in! Read Ephesians 6 and put on the whole armor of God!

Begin Prayer:

I now command all evil and demonic spirits: In Jesus' name, get up, get out, and go! Go to the feet of Jesus! (Repeat three or more times with a strong voice. Allow a brief pause to allow time for release. If there is no immediate release, understand they will have to go and maybe over a time period of days.)

Now, dear Father God, I ask humbly for the blood of Jesus Christ, Your Son and my Savior, to cleanse me from all these sins I have confessed and renounced, to cleanse my spirit, my soul, my mind, my emotions, and every part of my body that has been affected by these sins, in the name of Jesus Christ.

I also command every cell in my body to come into divine order now and to be healed and made whole as they were designed to be by my loving Creator, including restoring all chemical balances and neurological functions, controlling all cancerous cells, and reversing all degenerative diseases. I sever the DNA and RNA of any mental and/or physical diseases and/or afflictions that came down through my family blood lines. I also ask to receive the perfect love of God that casts out all fear, in the

Jesus 911

name of the Lord Jesus Christ.

Lord Jesus Christ, I am asking You to circumcise my heart (Hebrews 4:12), to increase Your love within me. I desire to be obedient and to embrace humility. I ask for Your help to submit to the complete will of God. I desire to live a righteous life so I can delight in the Lord with faith, sincerity, security, reverence, and forgiveness of others. Let my hands be holy and increase my confidence as your child.

I also ask You, Lord, to fill me with Your Holy Spirit now according to the promises in Your Word. I take to myself the whole armor of God in accordance with Ephesians 6 and rejoice in its protection as Jesus surrounds me and fills me with His Holy Spirit. I enthrone You, Lord Jesus, in my heart, for You are my Lord and my Savior, the source of eternal life. Thank You, Father God, for Your mercy, Your forgiveness, and Your love, in the name of Jesus Christ, Amen.

Note: Now, through communion, enter into covenant with the Lord by taking of the Lord's bread and wine.

Section Two

Chocolate Covered Demons

How did this happen? I've gone to church all my life. How can I have a demon? If I have a demon, how do I know and how can I get rid of it? These are the questions that Larry and I often hear. Many times, people do not recognize (or choose not to recognize) or justify their sin because it doesn't appear to be "that bad." They might say something like, "It was just a little money, and they will never miss it" in an effort to justify stealing. Satan uses justification to lie to you. He hides your sins so that he can gain power over you. He covers them up in different ways to make them acceptable, "You deserve to feel love. You've earned it. No one will ever know." These lies cover the demons (in chocolate) to make them acceptable to us. They are not hidden from Jesus.

There are all kinds of chocolate, just as there

are all kinds of sin. There is milk chocolate, dark chocolate, white chocolate, bitter chocolate, powdered, hard, or chips. Chocolate's decadent taste and appeal is used as a stimulus for our emotions. Thus, we decide that anything with chocolate makes us feel loved, wanted, justifiable, able to handle our loneliness. Covering our sin up can create emotional weights through bitterness, distrust, unforgiveness, fear, pride, ungodly soul ties, or unworthiness. In other words, we think chocolate cures everything. And in the same way, Satan makes us think that sin cures everything.

We are born with an innate understanding between right and wrong. Our choices put into motion blessings or consequences. Satan prowls around like a roaring lion just waiting for us to make the wrong choice that will release the gate for demonic spirits. Satan is a liar. We would not believe the lie if it weren't mixed with a little truth. You will find there is usually 90% truth in every lie. Our natural reactions to sins are to lie about them and keep them a secret so that no one will know or judge us. Thus, we justify and hide our sins by covering them with—chocolate. When this happens, Satan has a legal right to set in place his demons of torment.

When your faith becomes greater than your fear, God will dictate your destiny, not satan.

Prayer is a key to unlocking the prison bars that keep you captive to feelings of hopelessness and desperation. The following prayers will empower you to break Satan's legal right to you. Be assured that Satan will not give you up easily. His interest and attention are on those who want to be free, not the ones he is holding captive by their own choice.

Exercising Your Spirituality

During this next section, Larry and I will empower you with prayers to exercise your spiritual authority (by using the power of Jesus' name) through repenting, renouncing, and reclaiming your life. Evil spirits are present where there are iniquities, transgressions, sins, and diseases. Many believe that Christians cannot be subject to oppression by Satan's authority. However, our years of personal experience in deliverance proves otherwise. Christians still sin and open doors to demons after they come to faith in Jesus. Demons, devils, and unclean spirits are not limited by religion, people group, gender, believers, or nonbelievers. Mark 7:21–23 reads, "For from within, out of the heart of men, proceed evil thoughts, adulteries, fornications, murders, thefts, covetousness, wickedness, deceit, lewdness, an evil eye, blasphemy, pride, foolishness. All these evil things come from within and defile a man" (NKJV).

Jesus paid for all our sins on the cross, His resurrection power gave eternal life in heaven to those who believe He is the Son of God. He took every curse and disease, but not the consequences of our of sin. The repentance of sins is what gives us—*freedom.*

Joe Allbright explains biblical freedom best when he writes:

Jesus Christ gave us our ability to walk in the freedom He intended, and to have peace and joy in our heart. This depends on our willingness to surrender every area of our life to Him (including wounds of the past). True freedom is not the freedom to do what we want, when we want. True freedom is the ability to bring every area of our lives under the direction and control of Jesus Christ. We desire to help you identify areas of your life that have not been surrendered and that are keeping you from walking in the freedom God has intended for you (Allbright, Joe. *Liberating the Bruised*. J.E. Allbright, 1997).

Sadly, approximately 75% of the problems Christians experience are related to lack of acknowledgement of their sin, forgiveness, vows, judgments, generational curses, and spoken curses. As we journey through each section, Larry and I will provide you with definitions, examples, prayers for freedom, and biblical references. Before we begin the prayer, please consider the following:

- Speak all prayers and responses aloud and in Jesus' name. (Note: God *spoke* the world into existence; there is power in the spoken word.)
- Jesus gave us the authority to use His

name. James 2:19 says, "You believe that there is one God. You do well. Even the demons believe—and tremble!" (NKJV).

- Have someone with you that you feel you can trust. We recommend that it be someone other than your spouse or a parent.
- The Holy Spirit may bring something to remembrance that you need to work through.

Legal Deliverance

When an individual commits sin, they give legal right to demons to come in or upon them. This includes generational demons that come against someone because their ancestor(s) didn't ask for forgiveness from the Lord, didn't ask the Lord to break the rights of the demons from their lives, and didn't bless themselves and their following generations. There are several areas of prayer in this section; breaking soul ties, removing iniquities, transgressions, sins, and bitterness.

In the following section we provide you with prayers that you can pray to break curses. These prayers are effective. Through the grace of Jesus, your faith, your trust in Him, your humility before God the Father, and your total honesty, these prayers will give you more freedom in life than you have experienced. Often, we are asked if this will break the curse off my children. Our belief is that the answer depends on the age of the child. We believe it does break the curse off your children if they are under the age of accountability (age 12 scripturally). If they are over 12 and under your authority, then include their name in the prayer as you come before the Lord. Adult children need to understand and pray for themselves, and a spouse needs to pray the prayers for themselves.

Legal Deliverance Prayers

Deliverance and healing through prayer is essential to getting your freedom from demonic spiritual oppression. Most of us are not aware that in over 30% of the recorded biblical Scriptures when Jesus healed someone, He also delivered them from demons. Jesus gives us charge to "Heal *the* sick, raise *the* dead, cleanse *the* lepers, cast out demons. Freely you received, freely give" (Matthew 10:8, NASB).

The following prayers systematically destroy the *legal rights* of demons to inflict sickness, torment, and life difficulties (poverty, addictions, fear) against you. Through these prayers you will break the vows, judgments, unforgiveness, bitterness, wounding, and sinful soul ties of the past and present.

Jesus would have gone through all of this if it had only been YOU that would receive salvation.

You will find healing, freedom, and deliverance when you truly forgive in a deeper way those you have only given surface levels of forgiveness. "Jesus said, 'Father forgive them, for they do not know what they are doing'" (Luke 23:34, NIV).

Jesus was the ultimate sacrifice. He suffered beatings, bruising, humiliations, mocking, poverty, abandonment, fear, and anxiety to the point of sweating blood, and ultimately, He *died on the cross just for us*. Jesus would have gone through all of this if it had only been *you* that would receive salvation. It is hard to understand that level of forgiveness. We can only hope to achieve it. We must try.

The root of bitterness grows from unforgiveness. This root of bitterness must be cut and burned away. Bitterness from your own unforgiveness is one thing, but we have found that often bitterness from someone else's unforgiveness is taught to others or taken on because of wounding or generational unforgiveness. "For I see that you are in the gall of bitterness and in the bondage of [generational] iniquity" (Acts 8:23, ESV). Take some time and think about the areas of your life where bitterness has taken residence.

Note: You may want to make a list. During the prayer to destroy bitterness, specifically ask for the cutting away of the roots of bitterness and the destruction of every limb, branch, twig, and seedling.

Example: A woman is disappointed in life, many times by men. Her anger led to unforgiveness that progressed to bitterness toward all men. She loves her children and works two jobs to provide for them. She wants to be married to a kind, honest, dependable man who cares for her and would support her and the children. Never finding this, she becomes more and more bitter. Later, she speaks negative and harsh words against her children's and grandchildren's spouses. She has now *taught* them bitterness through her words and actions. "Only depend on yourself," she tells them, or, "I would never tolerate that behavior; you should leave him." These words are very damaging, but the children believed differently, and every marriage remained together through love and respect.

Breaking Agreement With Demonic Spirits

Your verbal prayers will help you break agreement with demonic spirits including familiar spirits operating in your life. Evil spiritual rights and schemes of the enemy are broken when you believe in Jesus. "Confess your sins to each other and pray for each other so that you may be healed" (James 5:16, NIV). Then, with a broken and contrite heart renounce and repent for them, forgive and bless others, and submit yourself to the Lord. Ask the Holy Spirit to reveal the areas of your spirit and soul where the enemy has operated (entry points) so that you can be healed and set free. When you command all demonic presences to leave, they must obey because you are praying and speaking with the authority Jesus Christ gave you in His name. However, it is imperative that you are completely truthful regarding any sin, past or present. Accept responsibility for your sins, your transgressions (when you fall back into the same sin), and your family iniquities (the sins of your ancestors). You may have asked for forgiveness, confessed your sins, and repented to Jesus, but *He already knew*, and He wants you healed and free. Find someone you are willing to be totally open with and *confess*! Don't worry about being judged. Be honest. *Be free!*

Finding a support group or someone available for prayer and encouragement is important as you walk out your deliverance and inner healing. After praying, you may feel physically different instantly or within a few hours. You might even experience brighter vision, like a weight has been lifted off, or clearer thinking and focus. Additional release and deliverance may be experienced for several days after the prayer ministry through such things as yawning, tearing, ears popping, and nausea.

Be watchful! After prayer the enemy will lie to you "that you are not worthy" or "that you didn't receive your deliverance." Don't believe his lies. The demons are just waiting for you to give them the right to come back. Be strong and fight back! Control your thoughts and remember who you are. You are a child of the Most High God. Read and memorize James 4:7, Isaiah 54:17, and Ephesians 6:10–18.

Be sure to walk close to the Lord through regular Bible reading, church attendance, Christian fellowship, and prayer. Beware that the enemy will tempt you with the very thing that allowed the demon a legal right to you before.

Example: If you were delivered from lust, the enemy will tempt you to look at pornography that might just pop up on your computer screen or convince you that going to a gym and looking at the women in their workout apparel is alright (anything to create lustful desire). You will have spiritual warfare, but press in. Stay determined!

With Jesus you can resist and overcome. "Father God, Lord Jesus Christ, and Holy Spirit, I have come to receive ministry, deliverance, and healing in all parts of my spirit, soul, and body according to Scripture (Matthew 18:18; John 16:23) and to acknowledge that You, Lord Jesus, have given me the power and authority to use Your name for this purpose. I identify myself as Your child and by the name I have been given on earth (state out loud all names you have been known by, including your full birth name, married name, adopted name, and nicknames) _____ _____."

Prayer to Establish the Atmosphere

Begin Prayer:

Our Father, thank You for loving me and calling me by name before I was formed in the womb. Thank You for having high and holy purposes for me even before I was born. I give You praise, honor and glory for all that You have done, are doing, and will do for my good. I ask You to bless me as I begin. Holy Spirit, reveal any unforgiveness in me and remind me of anything I have chosen to forget. Lord, cut and break away from my life forever all curses, vows, judgments, roots of bitterness, and ungodly soul ties.

I take the authority given to me by Jesus Christ and command all demonic evil and unclean spirits, including all evil spirits that are empowered by curses and/or controlled by curses under Satan's authority and control, that they shall not interfere with me spiritually, mentally, or physically. You will not cause any pain or any fear in all parts of my spirit and soul (saved and unsaved), including both the inside and outside of my body. You shall not cause any confusion, slumber, sleep, restricted verbal communications or physical distractions including pain.

I command all that are under Satan's authority to stop and desist now. You will stand down and not hinder my free will or this time of prayer, repentance, and deliverance. I release any and all previously bound evil spirits and all that have no legal right to me to leave and go to the feet of Jesus now. At any time during my prayers, if your name is called, your function or purpose is named, or legal right is broken, you will immediately leave me and go to the feet of Jesus. As you leave, you will relinquish your influence over me that you have used to reinforce the Strong Man. I now bind the Strong Man with a three-cord rope that is not easily broken, from the top of his head to the bottom of his feet, to be tied where he can't get loose. He is to be blinded and gagged and will no longer have authority over me and my generations. He shall not intimidate or sacrifice any that are under his control, and he will be stripped of all influence and the legal rights to possess me and my family. The Strong Man will identify himself by showing his bound hands, give his name, purpose, and immediately go to the feet of Jesus to become His footstool, or to the pit when commanded.

I declare the kingdom of God is and shall be established here on earth as it is in heaven at this time and this location. "Your kingdom come, / your will be done, / on earth as it is in heaven" (Matthew 6:10 NIV). Lord, I have come to do the business of Your kingdom and to do violence to the kingdom of Satan.

Prayer to Establish Protection

Begin Prayer:

I thank You Lord for protecting me, for Your mercy, for Your son Jesus Christ, for Your word, and for Jesus' blood atonement upon the cross. I plead the blood of Jesus Christ

- over everyone here today;
- over all parts of my spirit, soul, and body;
- over the door posts and thresholds, over this place;
- over my loved ones, family members, extended family, my animals;
- over my transportation and all good gifts from the Lord.

I thank You Father for Your Holy Spirit and for the anointing that breaks the yoke so the captives can be set free. I submit to the Holy Spirit and ask the Holy Spirit for help to reveal all things necessary for the freedom promised by Jesus Christ for *me*. I thank You Father for Your holy angels. I ask that You station Your warring angels and Your ministering angels here to help with this deliverance.

Prayers of Boldness Against Satan

Begin Prayer:

Satan, I address you in the name of Jesus Christ, who is my Lord. I speak to

- the principalities and powers;
- the rulers of the darkness of this age;
- the spiritual hosts of wickedness in heavenly places;
- the demons, the devils, evil and unclean spirits ;

- fallen angels and/or any other names or titles you have taken upon yourselves or have been given.

I declare my Lord Jesus Christ has totally conquered you

- at the cross when He triumphed over you;
- when He held you up to public ridicule.

My Lord now has all authority and all power in Heaven and on earth. He has given me the authority to use His name.

In Jesu's name I speak to all that are under Satan's authority and control. I command you

- not to manifest, blaspheme and lie;
- not to communicate with each other;
- not to communicate with any entity above, below, and around you;
- to disentangle yourselves from one another;
- not to hold hands and you cannot hold

onto each other;
- to turn loose of each other now;
- to line up and leave when I command, dismiss, and release you;
- to leave when your purpose or function is repented of.

You will immediately leave this area and go to the feet of Jesus to become His footstool or wherever I direct. You shall never return to me and my dwelling place.

Releasing the Freedom of Jesus Christ

The Lord already knows your sins. If you have repented and asked for forgiveness, then the Lord has forgiven you. However, if you have not followed the process of James 5:16, "Confess your sins one to another, and pray for one another so that you may be healed" (NASB), then the demons still have a claim to you and will try to lead you back into the same sin. Deliverance from the evil spiritual world is only *part* of what the Lord wants for you. He also wants you healed.

Demons Still Have a Claim to You

For the following prayers, boldly speak out and confess your sins so that the legal rights of the demons are destroyed. Also, it is essential that you maintain a humble attitude. Psalms 51:17 reads, "A broken and a contrite heart— / These O God, You will not despise" (NKJV).

Before you begin this next section, pray and ask the Holy Spirit to reveal to you any and all sins you may have forgotten or repressed.

Prayer of Identification and Repentance

Begin Prayer:

Father God, I love You, and I know You love me. Please help me with my unbelief and forgive me for not receiving Your unconditional love like a child. Please change me. I invite *Jesus* into my heart to do everything He needs to do in all parts of my spirit, soul, mind, and body so that I may be healed and set free.

I give Jesus permission to do anything He needs to do in order to help heal my pain and remove my scars. Today, I need a miracle from You. Lord Jesus, heal my hurts, remove my scars, and fill my vacant places with Your Holy Spirit.

I renounce, I repent, and I ask forgiveness for myself and the inequities of my fathers and forefathers; also my mother and her family back to Adam and Eve, including:

- Demonic oppression from the evil one in our lives
- Self-curses, family spoken curses, ritual curses, curses by others, ingested curses, and biblical curses because we have violated the word of God
- Killing, torturing, maiming, hurting and/or abusing people verbally or

financially
- Demonic contracts, blood contracts, and dedications made to Satan and all that are a part of his kingdom
- False religions, secret organizations, occult practices and witchcraft that has attached to and encumbered our family bloodline back to Adam and Eve

I humbly repent for my sins, my transgressions, and my inequities, including:

- Blood guilt (spilled innocent blood, abortion, murder)
- Immorality (illegitimacy, rape, incest, sexual perversion)
- Blood dedications and contracts and agreements with Satan
- Participating in ungodly organizations
- All types of idol- and self-worship
- False religion, demonic and occult worship (Freemasonry, Satanism,

Buddhism, Hinduism, Islam, Eastern Star, Catholicism, Unity, New Age, Bhai, Islam, and _____(other))
- Occult practices
- Self-mutilation (cutting, piercing, tattoos, eating disorders)
- Ignorance of the Word of God and His truth
- Illegal drugs and the abuse of pharmaceutical drugs
- Compulsive habits; smoking, drinking of alcohol, stealing, gossip, gluttony, overspending, hoarding, excessive cleanliness, pharmaceutical and recreational drugs
- (Other)_____

Lord, I ask You for complete release and cleansing through the blood of Jesus Christ.

And, I repent of every sinful attitude, including:

- Lustful thoughts and desires

- Pornography and sexual perversions
- Vain imaginations and fantasies
- Irresponsibility and manipulations
- Selfish desires and ambitions for power and domination
- Co-dependency, being judgmental, and pride
- Doubt, distrust, rebellion, and anger
- Fear, rejection, and unforgiveness
- Bitterness and mockery

I repent for any actions or habits that did not glorify God. And I repent of any spoken vows, judgments, curses, or gossip that did not glorify Jesus Christ. I ask for forgiveness, release, cleansing, and wholeness.

I renounce Satan and all demonic influences in my life, including:

- Bondages and dominations
- Accidents and infirmities
- Depression and poor self-esteem

- Confusion and unjustified guilt

Lord, I ask for the release and freedom promised by Jesus Christ so that He may be Lord of my total humanity and be glorified in all I say and do.

PERSERVERANCE

Let me congratulate you on the hard work you have done so far. It took a lot of courage and fortitude, but you are making lasting change for yourself and your family. Our next prayer is the *Divine Exchange*. Don't believe the enemy's lie that you have done all you can. *Instead, press on*!

Instructions For The Divine Exchange

Take a minute and quiet yourself. Breathe deeply. Realize God the Father, the Lord Jesus, the Holy Spirit, and heavenly angels are with you. Now, close your eyes and imagine a large white sheet lying flat at your feet. This next prayer will lead you to place many things in the sheet. However, as you pray you may think of other things you want to add—then do it! Also, don't rush this process. This is your time. Be humble and sincere. These prayers are not just ink on paper or casual words. They have power and authority because it is done in Jesus' name with His power and authority and the authority He gave you.

Prayer For Cleansing Through the Divine Exchange

Begin Prayer:

Lord Jesus, since You paid for my sins, I will bundle them up and lay them at Your feet. When I leave this room, *I am not going to take any of them with me.* In my mind's eye, I will now prepare my bundle in a white sheet I place before me. (Pause and visualize what you are doing.)

In my bundle, I give Jesus the guilt, the fears, the condemnations, the judgments, the shame, the curses, all penalties (you might want to add things like anxiety, depression, sorrow, manipulations).

(Take your time.)

I take the opposite corners of the sheet and tie them together in a knot and take the other two corners and tie them together. Now, I tie the corners into one knot. Lord Jesus, I'm ready to give this heavy bundle to You. Forgive me Lord for trying to carry it myself. I am not going to insult You by picking up what You paid for. These sins will no longer be mine, so I abandon them to You. Thank you Lord. In Jesus' name, Amen.

"Take my yoke upon you and learn from me, for I am gentle and humble in heart, and you will find rest for your soul. For my yoke is easy and my burden is light" (Matthew 11:29–30, NIV).

Prayer of Release from Anger

The purpose is to receive release from anger towards the Deity, breaking vows, and breaking judgments.

Note: Before our next prayer, you must come to terms with any anger you may have toward God and others—especially parents and authorities. Make a list of those you have anger

toward. Be honest with yourself. The Lord already knows, and if possible write why you are angry, even why you are angry with your heavenly Father, Jesus, or the Holy Spirit.

Begin Prayer:

I now come to the cross to repent and renounce my words of anger toward my Heavenly Father, Jesus Christ, and the Holy Spirit. I repent for blaming You for the bad things and suffering that I have endured. I now know that You work all things for good, and it was Adam and Eve that chose this direction for us all. I ask You to forgive me for all vows and judgements that were spoken by me toward _____(speak out the first names and the reason) _____ and others in anger, using the Lord's name in vain and manipulation. I ask You to forgive me, and to cover me with the blood of Jesus Christ.

According to Your word, "No weapon formed against you [me] shall prosper, / And every tongue *which* rises against you [me] in judgment / You shall condemn. / This *is* the heritage of the servants of the Lord, / And their righteousness *is* from Me, Says the Lord" (Isaiah 54:17, NKJV). I condemn and I ask the Lord also to condemn the tongue that has raised up against me or that I used in anger to come against others. With the sword of the Spirit, I now break and cut away all words of anger spoken against me in vows and judgements.

I also break and cut away all words of anger, vows, and judgements I have spoken against others, including:

- Any authoritative persons that have been over me
- Ancestral fathers and mothers back to the generation of Adam and Eve
- Biological father, biological mother, adopted parent(s) and/or stepparent(s)
- Spouse, (ex-spouse), children, and siblings

- Relatives, friends, and people that have hurt/betrayed me
- Physicians, lawyers, employers, teachers, church leaders
- Warlocks, shamans, witches, including all under Satan's influence, authority, and control

Lord Jesus, I choose to forgive all those who have come against me. I renounce my anger, and I repent. I ask You to bless them, and I bless them.

In Jesus' name.

Note: Take your time through this process. Ask the Holy Spirit to bring back to your remembrance the names of those you may not think of at this time. It is common that these names will come when you least expect them too. When that occurs, simply renounce your anger, forgive them, and bless them.

Iniquities, Transgressions, and Sins

Begin Prayer:

In the name of Jesus Christ and with the sword of the Spirit I now break and cut away all demonic legal rights, including ancestral and familiar spirits to any and all parts of my spirit, my soul, and my body, including:

- Demonic assignments, curses, and schemes
- Demonic soul-ties
- Generational demons attached to curses and iniquities of our fathers and forefathers (including my mother's side) back to Adam and Eve
- My personal sins, transgressions, and iniquities.

I repent for the following and all that are categorized as a part of them:

- Infirmities: hereditary diseases, cancer, diabetes, heart disease

- Lust, sex, and idolatry: adultery, fornication, pornography, homosexuality, perversion
- Fear and rejection: abandonment, insanity, anxiety, inadequacy, loneliness, insecurity
- Death and heaviness: confusion, depression, abortion, discouragement, hopelessness
- Rebellion: doubt, distrustful, stubbornness, unbelief, anti-authority, passivity
- Pride: intellectual pride, arrogant, controlling, dictatorial, manipulative, vanity, legalistic
- Religious experiences: Catholicism, Jehovah's Witness, New Age, Satanism, Native American
- Unforgiveness: distrustful, anger/wrath, bitterness, hatred, violence, jealousy

- Lies you have believed: Poor self-image, stupid, you're ugly, whore, you're unwanted
- Occult, divination, and witchcraft: astronomy, fortune tellers, Tarot cards, hypnosis
- Slumber and sleep: constant fatigue, procrastination, success blocked, passivity
- Error: confusion, doubt/unbelief, irresponsibility, immaturity, justifying sin
- Bondage and binding: eating disorders, continuous immorality, chemical addictions
- Anti-Christ spirit: denies Jesus as Savior, blasphemes the Holy Spirit, opposes the Bible
- Thoughts, attitudes, and idols of the heart: evil thoughts, doubt, racism, resentment
- Items related to curses: Making and losing money, selfishness, deify deity, emotional

Lord, I ask You to forgive any generational sins and iniquities back to Adam and Eve. I ask You to forgive me of all undenounced sins, transgressions, thoughts, attitudes, idols, vows, and judgments that I have committed that were not mentioned and all items associated and connected with the categories just spoken.

I ask You to break, cut away, cast down, make null and void, and to remove the penalties, including any death assignments and death spirits. I ask You to apply the blood of Jesus Christ to me so that I may be cleansed and redeemed.

Declaration

The purpose of this declaration is to command evil spirits to leave.

Begin Declaration:

I declare my right to stand in the presence of the Most High, no longer hindered in any way by the previous generations or myself by words, curses, hexes, spells, contracts, blood covenants, and incantations from any source. Thank You Lord Jesus Christ! Amen!

Begin Prayer:

I dismiss and command the Strong Man and all evil spirits, unclean spirits, and demons attached to or connected in any way, to all vows, judgments, and every item mentioned in all categories. You are now released and dismissed to go immediately to the feet of Jesus to become His footstool. In Jesus' name, g et up, get out, and go! Go to the feet of Jesus! (Repeat three or more times with a strong voice. Allow a brief pause to allow time for release. If there is no immediate release, understand they will have to go and maybe over a time period of days.)

I now let and release the holy angels to torment all evil spirits, demons, and unclean spirits and intensify the torment until all have left.

The Choice

Forgiveness is a choice, and it's critical to your freedom and healing. A synonym for forgiveness is *absolution*. You cannot forgive only a part of the offense, the hurt, or anger. Forgiveness must be absolute and final. The more you carry unforgiveness, the more it will grow like a cancer, lingering and spreading pain. If you have ever said, "I will never forgive them," then you have cursed yourself and will continue to feed the destructive cancerous curse. In addition to this, unforgiveness manifests as chronic illnesses passed from generation to generation, broken relationships, and bitterness. Forgiveness requires a humble heart and sometimes a personal encounter to ask the person to forgive you for your unforgiveness. They may not be aware of your offense. I can speak to this from personal experience and can tell you it was very healing. Unforgiveness, anger, bitterness, and deceit inflict pain in your soul, causing more hurt and torment to you than to the other person.

Unforgiveness stems from anger or disappointment. It is okay to be angry, however, we are not to let the sun go down on our anger (Ephesians 4:26). This is usually not the case. Anger just festers and grows, and then we tell someone else, getting them to support our anger and unforgiveness, and then tell someone else. It is important to direct your anger to the demonic cause of the anger, hurts, and oppression, which will free you to forgive the person, who is also a victim. It is important that you release all emotional strongholds and that you forgive every person who has hurt you and their actions. The four basic steps of forgiveness are confess, repent, forgive, and bless.

You must repent and forgive everyone in the same way Jesus has forgiven us. There are no exceptions. It is not enough just to say, "I forgive or I have forgiven them already" so that you may be forgiven. Forgiveness must be from the heart. "Be kind and compassionate to one another, forgiving each other, just as in Christ God forgave you" (Ephesians 4:32, NIV).

As He hung on the cross, Jesus modeled complete forgiveness from His heart because of His love for you (Luke 23:34).

Declaration to Forgive

Make a list of the first names and the offenses of those you know you need to forgive. If you cannot remember, ask the Holy Spirit to bring to mind anyone that you may have forgotten. At a later time, you may have someone else "pop" into your mind and at that time you can say the prayers of forgiveness for that situation and for the persons involved.

Ask the Lord to bless them and then earnestly pray a blessing for them. (Note: If you struggle with this part, ask the Lord to bless them. Ask the Lord to bless them with a closer relationship with Jesus.) Forgiveness is also required for trauma-induced memories that control our lives. We are not trying to simplify forgiveness. It's harder in some situations than others. Ask the Lord to help you. Jesus promises to be your strength in your weakness. Lastly, burn or tear up the sheet with the names and offenses.

Note: There are separate prayers of forgiveness for

- parents, stepparents, godparents, and adopted parents;
- siblings, grandparents, children, and blood relatives.

The purpose of this next prayer is to forgive, release, and bless all who have caused offense against you.

Begin Prayer:

Jesus, I confess my need to forgive because I need to be forgiven. I ask You to please have the Holy Spirit help me bring to remembrance any unforgiveness, resentment, anger, and hatred toward men, women, family, children, spouse, friends, employers, employees, churches, authority, or leadership. (Speak out the first or last names of these people and the offense.)

I now confess this unforgiveness as a sin and repent. I humbly ask You, Lord, to forgive me. I now forgive them, Lord. I ask You to bless them that they would know true salvation and intimacy with Jesus Christ.

Prayer for Father and Mother Wounds

Note: If applicable do father and mother in one prayer, or individually if necessary. We recommend that you pray this prayer even if they have passed on.

Begin Prayer:

Thank You, Lord, for the father and mother You chose for me. I know they made many mistakes knowingly and unknowingly. They were not taught properly in their own homes. That's why they didn't teach me. I forgive my father and mother for their choices in raising me. Lord, I ask that You completely restore a godly relationship between us.

Remove the scars. Bless and heal the wounds. Fill the wounds, scars, and vacant places with the Holy Spirit and with the love of the Lord. Thank You, Jesus.

Personal Forgiveness and Blessing

You have now forgiven all that you can remember. The weight and load is getting lighter already. You're beginning to see more clearly (literally). Something is changing, even if you can't describe it. There is one person left to forgive. *That is you!* Don't feel badly for the part you have played in unforgiveness or offenses. Forgiving yourself may be the hardest person to forgive. It's time to pray for yourself.

Begin Prayer:

Lord, would You now bless me with the desires of my heart that magnify Your purposes for my life. Forgive me as I forgive myself for (make another list if you need to)_____ , and I bless myself. (Include blessings that are appropriate or your special requests.)

Bitterness

You may not recognize that bitterness has become a natural part of your personality. You may not consider yourself bitter, but only miserable, resentful, or taken advantage of. However, bitterness is controlled by demons that want to destroy not only you, but those around you. Also, bitterness can be taught. For example, a woman has several bad marriages. The first signals that show another marriage is going to end are statements such as, "He's just as bad as . . . I'm not going to do anything for him . . . He takes advantage of me." Then the mother moves in with her daughter and begins to repeat these same phrases about her son-in-law.

This changes the daughter's attitude toward her husband. She begins to be critical of the man she fell in love with and who loves her. She stops talking about the good things he does; being active in church, attention to her, participating with the children, going to work every day, providing, taking care of the house and cars. She begins to repeat what someone else thinks about men. A bitter and critical spirit will destroy a marriage or at least make it miserable. It must be destroyed! It may be necessary to openly discuss this with the "bitter teacher" and put a stop to it.

The purpose of this prayer is to remove bitterness. Key verses include Colossians 3:19, "Husbands, love your wives and do not be harsh with them" (NIV) and Luke 17:6, "He replied, 'If you have faith as small as a mustard seed, you can say to this mulberry tree, "Be uprooted and planted in the sea," and it will obey you'" (NIV).

Begin Prayer:

With the sword of the Spirit I now cut, pull out, and remove all demons connected to the root of bitterness within me. I repent for my attitude and unforgiveness toward all men and women, husbands, wives, ex-spouses, children, church leaders, friends, family members, and anyone and anything that hinders my walk with Jesus Christ. Lord, I ask You to reveal any root of bitterness that I have so that I can circumcise my heart, repent, and change my ways, including my attitude. I will obey the Word of God. I now declare that the root of bitterness that is within me is to die, to be plucked up by the root and to be planted in the sea. Further, I command that any trunk, branch, limbs, twigs, seeds, or leaves of bitterness are to be burned, totally destroyed, and become ash under my feet—never more to take root. Thank You, Jesus. Amen!

Soul Ties

Soul ties give away a piece of one's soul, for good or for bad. Good soul ties would be those between a husband and wife, friendships between Christians, and parents with their child. However, there are demonic soul ties that open the doors to evil spirits. Demonic soul ties include:

- Sexual sins: fornication, adultery, pornography, homosexuality, lesbianism, molestation, premarital sex (even if you married later), ex-spouses, rape, incest. (Note: This is the foremost of all the soul ties. Not only have you made a soul tie with the individual; all other sexual sins of the other person are included because sexual sin is the transmission of blood and becoming one with the other person.) Matthew 19:5 reads, "And he said, 'This explains why a man leaves his father and mother and is joined to his wife, and the two are united into one'" (NLT).
- Bestiality: identify acts with animals exactly, then repent (no shortcuts), including watching on TV, movies, and internet.
- Evil companions: influence of familiar spirit-drugs, drinking, carousing, etc.
  - Companionships: ungodly acts;

recreational, social, business
  - Subordinate relationships: teachers, pastors, counselors
- Perverted/co-dependent family ties (cut apron strings)
- With the dead: extreme grieving (over three months) and prolonged mourning (over one year) give opportunity for the spirits of sorrow, grief, and loneliness to enter a person.
- Death through abortion or miscarriage
- Within the church: cliques (excluding others and causing division, including pastors and other church leaders)
- False religions and their symbolism: books, perverted Bibles, statues, idols, jewelry, tattoos, masks, Indian religious artifacts, carvings of wood, jade, stone
- The Occult: connecting to the demonic realm by trying to connect by words,

counsel, necromancy, séance, prayers, and physical ungodly actions. Joining with or paying a warlock, shaman, witch, fortune teller, following New Age beliefs, hypnotism, using a Ouija Board, astrology, and divination. Participating in handwriting analysis, blood covenants, demonic games (computer or other), satanic rituals including blood sacrifices (human /animal). (Note: treat each one individually. If there is or has been heavy involvement in the occult, special prayers may be necessary.)

Prayer for Breaking Soul Ties

Note: Before you begin your prayer, make a list of the first names and/or circumstances regarding your soul ties.

Begin Prayer:

Lord Jesus, I confess I am guilty of: _____
_____

- Sexual sins
- Bestiality
- Evil companions
- Perverted family ties
- Soul ties with the dead and extreme grieving
- Soul ties within the church
- False religion and symbolism
- The occult and divination

These were sinful, and I ask for Your forgiveness. I repent and renounce all ungodly and demonic relationships.

With the sword of the Spirit I cut away these ungodly soul ties from my life forever. As an act of my will, I choose to forgive and bless those that have hurt me. I now bless these individuals _____ (use your list) _____ with peace, salvation, and intimacy with You, Lord Jesus Christ. And I ask You to bless them and forgive them. Thank you, Jesus.

(Note: While we are not blessing the act, we can bless the individual and the victim.)

Lord, any sinful soul ties that were not mentioned here and now I ask You to break in Jesus' name. I cut and break away all soul ties that did not honor and glorify You. I now ask You to return to me that which I gave away in sin so that I may be whole and honor You. I send back all ungodly attachments and soul ties to them so they may be whole and have a closer relationship with You. Please establish only godly soul ties in me.

Thank You, Lord, that in Your sight I am now purged, cleansed, and purified of every demonic soul tie in my life.

Note: If you are married include the following statement: "I now give to my spouse all that I had previously given or had been taken away in sin, that we may truly become one. In Jesus' name, thank You, Lord. Amen."

Declarations and Removal of Evil Spirits

You must agree and declare verbally that you will *fall out of agreement* with any demonic spirits, including familiar spirits that have been invited in and/or operated within your life.

Checklist:

1. All sinful acts have been repented of:

Yes or No

2. The demons know they have been found out: **Yes or No**

3. The demons are no longer wanted:

Yes or No

4. The demons know they have been renounced: **Yes or No**

5. This verbal confession destroys all their legal rights to remain: **Yes or No**

Note: If your answered Yes to all 5 questions, you're ready to move on. If you answered No to any one of them, then go back to that section of prayer and repeat it.

Prayer of Authority

The purpose of this next prayer is to establish authority and to command evil spirits to leave.

Note: If someone is praying with you, you may want them to make this declaration with you. Also, you should be able to do deliverance on yourself when completed with this prayer ministry at any time by going back to the first three prayers and then the section you feel needs more deliverance.

Begin Prayer:

I declare, in the name, in the power, and in the authority of Jesus Christ, all iniquities, transgressions, and sins mentioned or not, repented of or not, are now forgiven and covered by the blood of Jesus Christ. It was done and completed at the cross. *I am* now a blood-bought child of God, and I am in His hands. No creature will snatch me out.

Lord Jesus, by the delegated authority and power You have given to use Your name, I command all demons, all unclean spirits, all evil spirits of infirmity, all assigned spirits that enforce curses inside and out, located in all parts of my spirit, soul, and body to immediately leave now.

You're commanded not to manifest, blaspheme, or lie. You are to leave now! You will leave this area and go straight to the feet of Jesus Christ to become His footstool--never to return! I let and release the warring and ministering angels to enforce this prayer as long as necessary by whatever methods of torture, torment, and smiting to all demons, unclean spirits, evil spirits, to remove them in all parts of me.

I declare, no longer shall there ever be any evil fruit from any and all demons, unclean spirits, spirits of infirmity, sickness, cancers, tumors, viruses, germs, diseases, heart and blood disorders, including high blood pressure. You are to immediately wither, to be expelled and flushed from my body (the temple of the Holy Spirit). I am swept clean in all parts of my spirit, soul, and body. I rebuke fevers, pains, and weakness. I command my body to come into perfect balance (chemically and electrically) and to be healed. In Jesus' name.

I now ask and release the Holy Spirit to flow throughout my heart, mind, body, soul, and spirit and to heal, bring together, and integrate all parts of me as designed by our Lord Jesus Christ. Amen.

Closing Instructions

If demons manifest and will not leave, interrogate them and ask their name and tell them to describe their purpose and function. Demand to know their legal right(s). Then repent of sins that allowed the legal right, ask for forgiveness from the Lord and declare the demon is not wanted, its rights have been broken, and they must go to the feet of Jesus now. You may have to remove any accursed objects in your possession, in your home, or on your property that have been dedicated to evil or any symbolism. (Example: Dream Catcher, items from foreign countries that may have been cursed by a false religion, including objects in the foundations or walls. You may also want to walk the boundaries of your property with a small amount of anointing oil on the soles of your shoes and declare the land is dedicated to the God of Abraham, Isaac, and Jacob. All other dedications are broken in Jesus' name.

When the legal rights of the demon that manifest are broken, then make the demon repeat one word at a time: I_____ (Name/function of demon) (example: anger). I, <u>anger,</u> renounce all rights and claims to _____, and I now go immediately to the feet of Jesus (Alternate: I now go immediately to the pit or you command the demon to go to the pit). You must be strong. Stand your ground; you are a warrior in the army of the Lord. Jesus wins! You win!

Closing Ministry

Anoint yourself with oil, pray for any special needs, and ask for blessings. Partaking of the Lord's Supper (communion) is important for the closing time of ministry. Ask the Holy Spirit to fill in the

Jesus 911

vacant places left inside you with joy, happiness, and grace, including blessings for the children and spouse.

Section Three

Introduction to Inner Healing For the Soul and Spirit

Inner healing is needed when trauma-induced memories influence and control behavioral patterns, while also affecting your walk with the Lord. Trauma can begin at the point of conception, in the womb, at birth, or in daily life. The purpose of inner healing ministry is to remove the scars of trauma while healing the pain located in the spirit and the soul. Further, we desire to stabilize the individual so they may retain the blessings that the Lord wants to give them, have a closer relationship with Jesus, and find their freedom and wholeness that will give them the strength to overcome the enemy's schemes against them.

Trauma experiences include:

- **Trauma 1:** is a _limited_ event (could be one or several incidences). This is usually addressed in the ministry of *Legal Deliverance*. Examples may include a onetime rape, accident, or beating. (Some in the trauma 1 category may require an individual appointment if legal deliverance does not resolve the painful memory.)

- **Trauma 2:** is an <u>extended</u> and <u>repeated</u> incident(s) over a long period of time (sexual abuse, cruelty, neglect). This type of trauma would indicate a bruised and/or broken spirit. (Fractures and cracks in the soul of those who experience traumas in the trauma 2 category often require individual appointments.)

Purpose

The purpose of inner healing ministry is to heal, merge, and remove the pain that was created by trauma(s) that happened in an individual's life. At the time of the trauma, a fracture or alter may be created to help carry the pain of the event. Traumatic events like early childhood molestation, rape, parents' divorce, being bullied or battered, beaten or tortured, rejected or unloved, or a near death experience are just a few examples of trauma.

Clients have called us in fear of hearing voices in their head, unexplained torment, or unusual behaviors. It can be caused by a demon or a curse. If you have broken the legal rights of the demons and broken the curses, then is it time to look for something different? A fracture for an alter that needs help, needs healing, needs love and protection. This is when we pray and look to the Lord for direction on building trust with the fracture or alter and how to help them find healing.

In merging the fractures and/or alters, they become "one" with the person again. There is a feeling of wholeness, release, and strength. It is a peculiar feeling to a person that has not experienced this because it is something they have not felt in a long time. After a few days we have been told that they can make quicker decisions, feel happier, a cloud has been removed, a weight lifted off, their marriage is better, relationships restored with family, and much more. Praise the Lord!

Through prayer and this book, Larry and I desire to help strengthen you so that in turn you will be strong enough to build the kingdom of God here on earth as it is in heaven. Psalm 33:11 reads, "But the Lord's plans stand firm forever; / his intentions can never be shaken" (NLT). We also must be aware that the enemy is scheming against you, so you must, "Put on all of God's armor so that you will be able to stand firm against all strategies of the devil. For we are not fighting against flesh-and-blood enemies, but against evil rulers and authorities of the unseen world, against mighty powers in this dark world, and against evil spirits in the heavenly places" (Ephesians 6:11–12, NLT).

If It's Not a Curse and It's Not a Demon, What Is It?

Inner healing is the process of healing, mending, and resetting the inner part of our spirit and soul, which often affects our physical body. Some of the most common terms in deliverance ministry to describe the elements of inner healing are *fractures* and *alters*, which are often referred to as multiple personalities in the secular world. Fractures and alters are created by a person's mind to hold the mental and emotional pain brought about by trauma(s) or sins.

Trauma-induced memories can become a stronghold within your soul or spirit. You may adapt to fractures (controlling/restraining the side effect), however, often the challenges of life bring you to the point that you can no longer ignore these areas of trauma. This is when people reach out for help. After they are treated with medications, therapy, counseling, or ignored without success, they cry out for spiritual help: *Jesus 911*!

Traditional approaches to trauma seldom address the root issues that have now opened doors for demons or evil spirits, fractures, or alters. Individuals who have experienced trauma and who are in need of inner healing feel imprisoned, unable to move forward with their lives, become suicidal. They experience sorrows, sexual attacking demons, face poverty, and express feelings of remorse and regret. Not only does Satan lie to the traumatized person, he also lies to the *fractures* and *alters*.

A *fracture* or *alter* may be afraid of demons they too have seen within a person. Our ministry method does not allow the demons to manifest or cause harm to the individual, and because of this safety net the fractures and alters are more willing to merge with the *core* person. Before you try an inner healing you need to be sure that the Breaking of Curses and Legal Deliverance has been done; this will remove most of the fracture's or alter's fears. They are also more willing to cooperate and merge since they have seen Jesus at work. Larry and I do not use hypnosis or theophostic methods by design. Simply put, inner healing is the emergence of your conscious mind aligning with your subconscious mind just as you do in sleep. When you sleep, your subconscious continues all life functions while allowing your conscious thoughts to be put into order. An example of this would be if you have a project that you just can't quite find the solution, and after sleeping you have the answer the next morning without working at it.

Fracture Identification

Take your hand and hold it in front of you with all your fingers tight against one another. Separate one finger from the other five. It is still a part of your hand but it is separated. This is what happens when you experience a trauma and a fracture is created. That part of you (the fracture) will remain the same age as when the trauma occurred, even if the trauma was a "one-time" occurrence.

Jesus 911

Healing Fractures

Ask any fracture that wants to come up and talk to you to come forward. A fracture can come as a thought and speak as though it is *you*. It is like your subconscious mind speaking instead of your conscious mind. When you recognize this, be kind and gentle with yourself. Try to keep your conscious mind from interfering or trying to figure out what is happening. You will hear and know everything that is being said. Just let your conscious rest (go on vacation). This is not hypnosis! You may need your prayer partner to lead you through this process, but they are not to give you their thoughts or impose what they see or think. It's alright for your prayer partner to ask questions such as, "What is your name_____? What do you do for _____? Do you need to forgive someone? Do you know Jesus like _____?" Always give positive affirmations and thank the fracture for helping _____. Ask if they know Jesus as their personal Lord and Savior or if they would like to (if needed, lead them in the salvation prayer; many fractures were too young to accept Jesus). Ask Jesus to come and show Himself to the fracture. Then ask the fracture if they see Him (they usually do), and ask what He is doing. You will get answers like "He is playing with the children." "He wants to hold my hand." "He says He loves me." It is important not to rush this process. You are working with the *soul*. Let the fracture tell you how it feels (tired, lonely, sad). Ask if it would like to be a part of the *whole* _____(person)_____again. You can also ask the fracture if there are others there with them. Give the fracture time to answer. Usually there are, and this will give you an idea of others that need to be helped. Receive this hurting part of your soul when the fracture answers *yes*. Next, say "I'm going to count to three, and when I do, you can merge with (me). You are wanted and needed to make me strong."

Fracture Example

I once had a client that had been molested at a young age and created a fracture to hold the pain.

I asked the fracture what her name was, and she answered, "harlot." (The client hears everything that is being said, but they must keep their conscious mind out of the way.) Then I proceeded in a gentle voice to tell her Jesus did not give her that name, and He would like to give her a new name. She agreed that she wanted a new name. I told her Jesus saw her as "precious," because the Bible says He sees little children that way. The fracture accepted that name (the women actually smiled) and said she wanted to know Jesus. She accepted Him as Lord and agreed to become one with the core person. Words and tears cannot express what a wonderful experience that was for both of us.

Fracture Example

A father's infant daughter contracted an illness that kept the child in the hospital for many months. He researched and researched trying to find something to help his daughter. She heard him say "I just don't know what I'm going to do for her." It was a cry of desperation from the father. However, the subconscious of the child fractured, feeling unwanted and unloved. The child recovered and life went on. As a teen and young adult she got into rebellion, had to move back home, became depressed, withdrawn, and suicidal. She once again overheard her father telling her mother "I just don't know what I'm going to do for her." The next day her father died from a heart attack, and there would be no reconciliation. The fracture had been reaffirmed as unwanted and unloved. During ministry the Lord showed her that her father was desperate to *help* her and how he had struggled to find a way to do something for her; how much he loved her. The fracture healed!

Alter Identification

Now look at your hand and see you have a front side and a palm side. One hand with two sides. Consider this as an "alter." The alter will have been created when the same trauma occurs multiple times or when an individual has experienced a variety of multiple traumas. Alters will be the same age as the core person. Alters will *feel* accountable for all the bad things that happened to the person, will carry the pain, will consider themselves responsible for the person's happiness, joy, success, or failure. They may be angry because the core person did not do what the alter wanted them to.

The alter will be more inclined to come forward and act opposite of the core person. For example, one day you love pepperoni pizza and the next day you can't stand it. Or you may be kind and loving one minute, and something triggers the alter and you flip into being harsh and angry (different responses to the same circumstance). Alters are much more difficult to merge, and you may need a professional deliverance minister, prayer partner, or physician to help you. If you ask if they are tired of doing all the work, they usually will say something like, "Yes I'm tired--they can't do without me. It's my responsibility." You must convince them that with Jesus the individual can do life without the alter. The alter can now merge with the person.

Don't let anything or anyone stop you from getting freedom. Alters and fractures can only be healed or merged, not cast out like a demon. Jesus wants you to be healed and whole. He is right there with you, and He will heal you.

Childhood Alters

Created entities, imaginary playmates or friends that continue into teen and adult years are childhood alters. We have also seen this when a child loses a family member to death and continues to grieve their loss or feels, "They are right here with me, watching over me." The individual may also talk with them as though they were there, especially a close grandparent. These childhood alters make the person feel safe, that they were the only one that loved them, or they were the only one that listened.

Alter Example

Once I had a women who had experienced deliverance ministry several times, however, she was still struggling for complete freedom. As we progressed with the ministry, her behavior changed and she began acting as though a demon was manifesting (the prayers command demons not to manifest or interfere). The Holy Spirit prompted me to ask, "Are you a demon?" The response, "Of course I'm a demon." Again I asked, "Are you a demon?" The response this time was, "I think so." I asked, "Who do you answer to?" The response was, "I don't know." At this point I was able to recognize it was an alter that knew how demons acted and thought it was a demon. The alter had been created from extreme abuse and abandonment. Jesus revealed Himself in a powerful way and healed her spirit. Her entire life came into focus, repentance, and freedom!

Alter Example

She followed the Lord. She was a kind wife and loving mother. This was how she performed in public. However, when she was alone, her sexual alter took over. When this alter took over, it wore seductive clothing, took lewd pictures, was adulterous, and loved pornography. As a child, this woman was groomed to be a prostitute in an occult. Her heart belonged to Jesus, but the alter grew more powerful, and she could not control it.

Her husband discovered her other life. Devastated, she called on Jesus and our deliverance ministers. The demons were cast out and sent to the feet of Jesus, and every curse that had been placed on her was broken. That wasn't enough. The alter had to be healed and come to know Jesus as Lord and Savior in order to merge with the Christian side of her. After her healing, she destroyed all the pornography, shredded the provocative clothing, asked her husband to forgive her, took responsibility for the sins, and severed adulterous relationships. Forgiveness of those who had groomed her for prostitution was the key for her healing. She repented of the sins of the alter and herself and asked the Lord for forgiveness, restoration, and mercy. Once this was complete, the core person was ready to receive the alter as themselves. This oneness of spirit, soul, and body was a wholeness she had never experienced!

Understanding Trauma

In this ministry, we have discovered that trauma-induced memories influence, affect, and control our behavioral patterns and our walk with the Lord. Trauma can begin at the point of *conception, in the womb, at birth, or any critical age ranges.* Thus, fractures and alters can be created at any time.

- Conception: conceived by rape, incest, near death of the mother
- Womb: unwanted by one or both biological parents, failed abortion, near death of the baby, difficult labor and birth
- Critical ages: Trauma during these age ranges can create fractures because the child is old enough to know good from

bad but cannot control the circumstances (3 to 4 years old, 8 to 10, and 13 to 15); abuse, abandonment, shame, etc.

Note: We minister to two basic types of trauma that create fractures, alters, and personality disorders (PTSD):

- Trauma 1: a *limited* time event (could be one or several incidences) such as the loss of a beloved family member or pet. There are a few identification factors that help recognize this fracture or alter; created entities, imaginary playmates, withdrawing from life. This is usually addressed in the ministry of *Legal Deliverance*. But some areas may require individual counseling.

- Trauma 2: an *extended* incident(s) over a long period of time (repeated harsh discipline, criticism, illness, sexual abuse). Bruised and broken spirit and

fractures (cracks) in the soul always require individual appointments.
- The legal deliverance prayers should address these points. However, if you are still struggling with any of them, then inner healing would be helpful. There may also be unforgiveness or issues that were not revealed during the legal deliverance.

Note: The following thoughts and attitudes can hinder your healing and should be addressed during Legal Deliverance:

- Confusion
- Abandonment
- Lack of knowledge about God
- Shame, guilt, fear
- Anger
- Knowledge
- Misery

- Deception/Clone
- Religious spirit
- Intellectual pride
- False salvation, unbelief
- Satanic ritual abuse
- Demonic programing

Biblical words that describe the need for inner healing within the Soul and or Spirit:

- Scattered
- Captured
- Oppressed
- Shattered
- Fragmented
- Double-minded
- Denial
- Imagination/Fantasy
- Bruised (Reed)
- Discouraged
- Self-Hatred

- Broken Heart
- Fragmented
- Break/Crushed
- Insanity

Secular words that describe the need for inner healing within the soul and/or spirit:

- Dissociative Identity Disorder (DID)
- Multiple Personality Disorder (MPD)
- Attention Deficit Disorder (ADD)
- Post-Traumatic Stress Disorder (PTSD)
- Obsessive-Compulsive Disorder (OCD)
- Anxiety Disorder
- Satanic Ritual Abuse (SRA)
- Bipolar Disorder (BD)
- Schizophrenia
- Sociopath
- Psychopath

Note from the Authors

You have had great courage to complete the prayers, to open your heart, to receive truth and light into your soul, and to know the healing power of Jesus in your life. We are excited for you and how the Lord is preparing you to be a "Kingdom Builder." Now please receive this blessing from the Lord and from us.

–Larry and Marion

Aaronic Benediction. Numbers 6:24-26

The Lord bless you and keep you.
The Lord make his face to shine upon you
And be gracious to you.
The Lord lift up his countenance upon you
And give you peace.
So shall they put my name upon the people of Israel,
And I will bless them. (ESV)

Larry and Marion Pollard, Senior Ministers/Founders of "Comfort Ye My People Ministries"

Contact information: www.cmpministries.org

www.ingramcontent.com/pod-product-compliance
Lightning Source LLC
Chambersburg PA
CBHW070614010526
44118CB00012B/1506